The Beatles

TIM HILL

PULTENEY
PRESS

Published by International Book Marketing Ltd
First published in 2009

Pulteney Press
1 Riverside Court
St Johns Road
Bath, BA2 6PD, UK

© Atlantic Publishing
Photographs © Getty Images

A catalogue record for this book is available from the British Library.
ISBN 978-1-906734-56-5

Printed in Indonesia

Above: April 5, 1963: The Beatles mark the release of their debut album, *Please Please Me*, by picking up a silver disk for the single of the same name. They had served a long apprenticeship on the north-west club circuit and in Hamburg. There had been many setbacks, and numerous line-up and name changes, but after signing to Parlophone in June 1962, the Beatles were on course for global stardom. Pictured with the Moptops at the ceremony is producer George Martin. .

Opposite: The Beatles on stage at the Majestic Ballroom, Birkenhead, April 10, 1963. They had just finished touring the UK as one of the support acts to Helen Shapiro. At the start of the tour, the boys opened the show; by the end, they were closing the first half, a much more prestigious slot. It was the same story when they went on the road that spring supporting Chris Montez, Tommy Roe and even the Big O – Roy Orbison. Audience reaction made the Beatles the effective headline act, irrespective of the billing.

Opposite: The Beatles pictured outside EMI Studios, Abbey Road, July 1, 1963. The group spent the day recording "She Loves You", which became their first million-selling single. As the country went "Yeah Yeah Yeah" mad, Liverpudlians bemoaned the loss of their favorite sons. The Beatles played the last of around 300 Cavern Club gigs on August 3 that year.

Above: The Beatles developed a number of strategies to avoid being mobbed on their way in and out of concert venues. For this show at Birmingham Hippodrome in March 1963 they try to pass themselves off as policemen.

Opposite: George records the mayhem at London Airport as the Beatles return home from their first overseas tour, a week-long trip to Sweden in October 1963. Among the witnesses to Beatlemania that day was Ed Sullivan, the influential host of America's top-rated talk show. Those chaotic scenes helped Brian Epstein's cause when negotiations for a spot on the *Sullivan Show* took place the following month.

Above: After drawing breath for 24 hours following their return from Sweden, the Beatles launched into yet another UK tour on November 1, 1963, their fourth of the year. These £300-a-night gigs represented a healthy increase on the early Cavern appearances, for which they were paid £5, and the bank balance was about to be swelled further following the November 22 release of their second album, *With The Beatles*. With advance orders of 300,000, the album hit the number on spot five days later.

Opposite: The Beatles rehearsing for their appearance at the prestigious Royal Variety Performance, which took place at the Prince of Wales Theatre on November 4, 1963. The boys were seventh on the 19-act bill, but as they rounded off their four-song set with a barnstorming rendition of "Twist and Shout", there was little doubt who were the stars of the show.

Above: Passing the cigarettes round in an off-duty moment. In the early days, the Beatles thought nothing of smoking and drinking on stage, practices that were banned after Brian Epstein became the group's manager in December 1961. Epstein also ditched the Teddy Boy leathers in favor of sharp suits as part of the move towards greater professionalism.

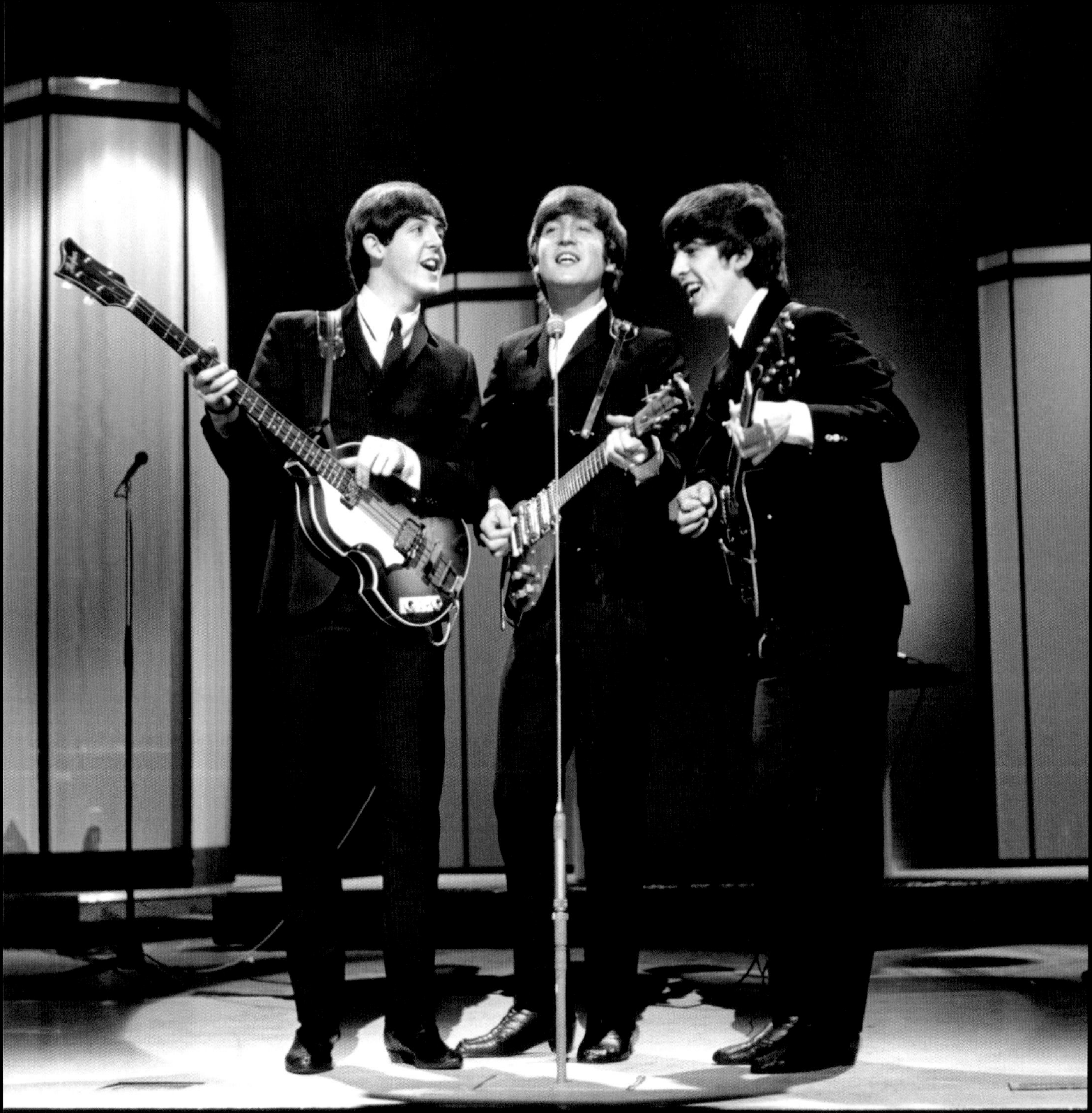

Opposite: Beatles shows in the early years often featured John, Paul and George singing close three-part harmonies around a single microphone. " This Boy", penned by John and released on the flipside of "I Want To Hold Your Hand" in November 1963, was a beautiful example of their three voices in mellifluous concert. To most groups it would have been A-side material, but the Beatles favored up-tempo numbers for their single releases.

Right: Paul became pigeon-holed as the sweet balladeer of the songwriting partnership, with John labeled as the hard rocker. It was a false assessment, for John was a master tunesmith in his own right, while Paul could rock with the best of them. On June 14, 1965, the day "Yesterday" was recorded, Paul also gave a bravura, raw rendition of "I'm Down", which was released on the B-side of "Help!".

Above: Another satisfied autograph hunter, this time on the streets of Paris. The Beatles' three-week
stay in France's capital early in 1964 proved to be a minor blip, Parisian audiences largely managing to
resist the infectious Beatlemania. Paris provided a watershed moment, however, as the Beatles learned
that "I Want To Hold Your Hand" had topped the American charts.

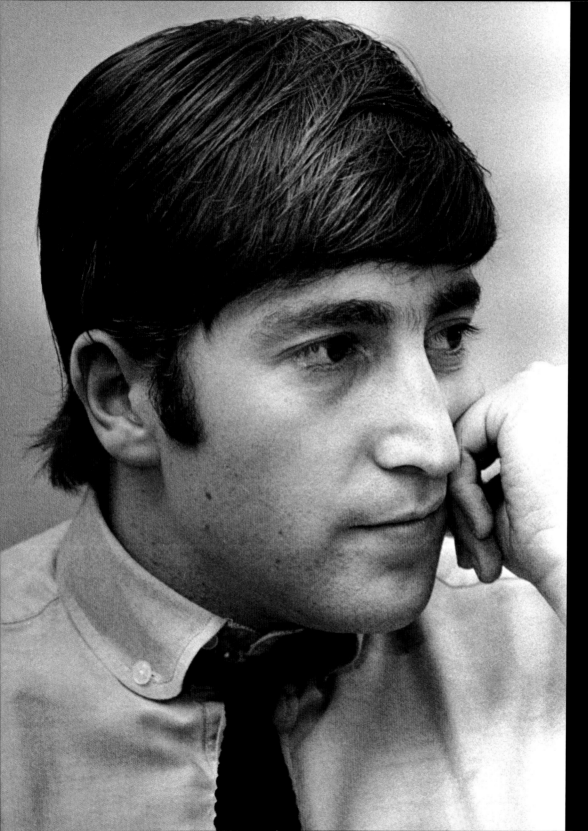

Left: John regarded the Beatles as his group, for it was he who had accepted Paul into the Quarry Men fold following their momentous meeting at Woolton Village Fete in July 1957. He recognized that Paul's talent might undermine his position, but was pragmatic enough to realize that with McCartney on board the group had more chance of making it big.

Opposite: John initially regarded Paul's young guitarist friend, George Harrison, as akin to an annoying kid brother. Once again, talent won the day, George's virtuosity on lead guitar getting him an entrée into the band in 1958. Four years passed before the immortal line-up was completed. Ringo was poached from rival Liverpudlian band Rory Storm and the Hurricanes in August 1962, replacing the axed Pete Best.

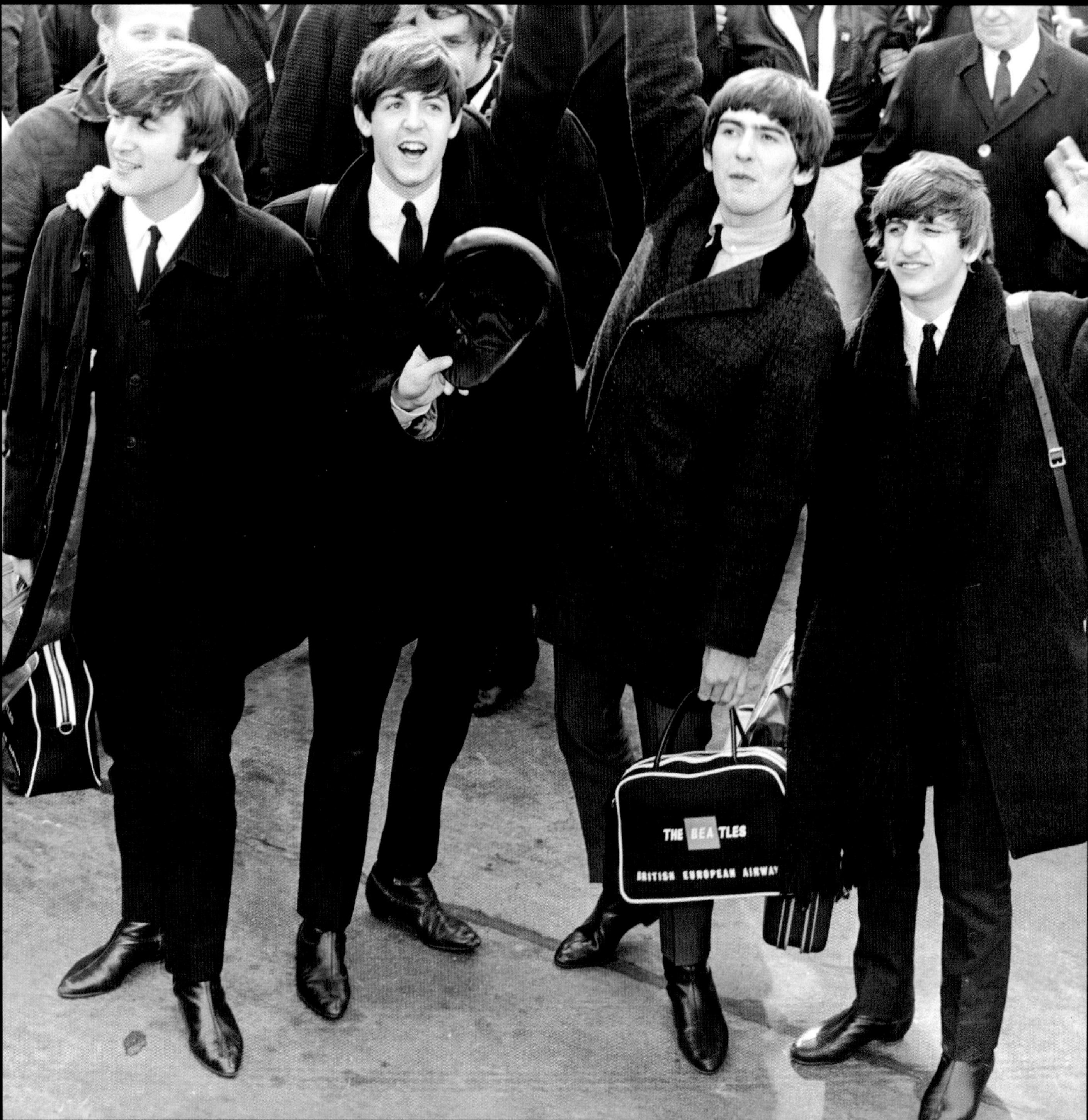
THE BEATLES

Opposite: The Beatles set out to conquer America on February 7, 1964. Much hype surrounded the trip – note the way that British European Airways incorporated their logo onto George's bag. Despite the publicity machine going into overdrive, and a number one record across the Pond, the Fabs were apprehensive about taking on America, which had been a graveyard for numerous British acts.

Right: The Beatles appeared live twice on the *Ed Sullivan Show* during their Stateside trip, attracting record television audiences of 70 million. Brian Epstein negotiated a modest $10,000 fee, as exposure on CBS's top-rated show was much more important than swelling the group's coffers.

Above: The Fabs played a five-song set on their first appearance on the *Ed Sullivan Show*: "All My Loving", "Till There Was You" and "She Loves You" in the opening half, followed by a rousing finale comprising "I Saw Her Standing There" and "I Want To Hold Your Hand". During rehearsals, George took ill and road manager Neil Aspinall stood in to allow the cameramen to set their positions. The future head of Apple enjoyed 15 minutes as a Beatle, George recovering in time for the following day's broadcast.

Opposite: In February 1964 "Beatlemania" swept New York and the boys weren't able to leave their hotel without police protection. The journey from New York to Washington had to be made by train and the police were on hand ensure their safety.

Above: In addition to their *Ed Sullivan Show* appearances, the Beatles played sell-out concerts at Washington Coliseum and New York's Carnegie Hall. The 8,000-strong Washington crowd easily drowned out the group's puny amplifiers, which totaled just 200 watts. Concerts would become scream-fests rather than musical events.

Opposite: The Beatles in casual attire during rehearsals for their second *Ed Sullivan Show* appearance, which aired on February 16, 1964. The boys had swapped a wintry New York for Florida sunshine, the show being broadcast from the Deauville Hotel in Miami. This time they played six songs, dropping "Till there Was You" and adding "This Boy" and "From Me To You" to the set.

Opposite and above: The Beatles played three concerts and made two TV appearances during their 15-day trip to the USA in February 1964. That represented a very light commitment compared with their usual punishing schedule, and it allowed the boys some welcome down time. Here they are pictured soaking up the Miami sunshine. By the time the Fabs flew home on February 22, the American public were in thrall. Records flew off the shelves so fast that in the first week of April the Beatles occupied the top five places on the *Billboard* Hot 100.

Opposite: On tour in Scotland, April 1964. The rapturous reception the Beatles received at the Glasgow and Edinburgh concerts was a far cry from the welcome they were given north of the border in May 1960, when as the Silver Beetles they toured as backing group to Johnny Gentle. On one occasion, they had been so hard up that they slipped out of a hotel in Forres without settling the bill.

Above: Politicians tried to curry favor with young voters by allying themselves to the greatest pop phenomenon in history. Prime Minister Alec Douglas-Home paid tribute to Britain's "best exports", while Labour leader Harold Wilson enjoyed a photo opportunity with the Fabs after presenting them with their Variety Club awards as Show Business Personalities of 1963 The luncheon ceremony took place at London's Dorchester Hotel on March 19 1964

Above: Hamming it up for the cameras during the group's short tour of Scotland, April 1964. The Beatles were hard at work on their third album, *A Hard Day's Night*, their first long-player comprising only self-penned songs. Side One provided the soundtrack to their debut feature film of the same name. United Artists had spotted that soundtrack albums were excluded from their EMI deal and wanted to get their hands on a valuable commodity. They got a cult film into the bargain!

Opposite: George and John photographed during the filming of *A Hard Day's Night*. George became increasingly frustrated at the supporting role he occupied within the group. "Don't Bother Me", which featured on *With The Beatles*, was the first Harrison song to make it onto an album, but it wasn't until the release of "Something" in 1969 that George took the

Opposite: By the spring of 1964, revenue from worldwide sales of Beatles records had reached a phenomenal £500,000 per month. The group's output was prodigious: four singles and two albums a year, concerts, countless media commitments – plus a debut movie feature.

Above: The Beatles' good looks and engaging personalities made them a big hit when they entered the acting stakes. Here they present Shakespeare, Fab Four style, with a spoof take on *A Midsummer Night's Dream*. The sketch was part of a TV special, *Around The Beatles*, which aired on May 6, 1964.

Opposite: The Beatles' first world tour, in summer 1964, brought a new contender for the title of "Fifth Beatle". When Ringo fell victim to a throat infection, Cockney session drummer Jimmy Nicol was drafted in as an emergency replacement. He deputized for gigs in Denmark, Holland, Hong Kong and the early dates in Australia, until Ringo took his usual place on the drum stool. His 11 days as a Beatle earned him £500 and an inscribed gold watch.

Above: Brian Epstein cut some poor deals for the Beatles, costing them millions, but his belief in the group when they were struggling to get a record deal cemented his place in their affections. When the boys received their MBE awards in 1965, George quipped that the acronym stood for Mr Brian Epstein.

Opposite: George influenced a generation of guitarists, particularly after he acquired a 12-string Rickenbacker during the trip to the States in February 1964. This was the instrument that produced the distinctive opening chord to "A Hard Day's Night". Byrds guitarist Roger McGuinn went out and bought the same guitar on the strength of it, while Gary Moore was another aspiring player who painstakingly tried to copy George's style.

Above: Ringo was a keen amateur photographer, and also the most talented actor of the four. He had more success with his efforts on both sides of the lens than when he tried his hand at songwriting. His "original" compositions often turned out to be subconscious copies of existing songs.

Opposite: On August 19, 1964 the Beatles embarked on a grueling month-long tour of the USA, criss-crossing the country by plane in a bid to satisfy the demand in 24 major cities. Kansas wasn't on the original schedule, but millionaire fan Charles Finley put up $150,000 for the Beatles to play an additional concert there. As the running time of the 12-song set was around half an hour, the band earned $5,000 a minute for the extra show.

Above: The price of success was virtual incarceration. When they weren't performing, the Beatles were cooped

Left: When George married Pattie Boyd in January 1966, Paul was the sole remaining single Beatle, the most eligible bachelor in the land. Many predicted wedding bells for Paul and Jane Asher, his girlfriend since 1963, but there were strains in the relationship. Jane had her own successful acting career, which meant enforced lengthy separations, and she never embraced the drug culture.

Opposite: John pictured with his wife Cynthia and son Julian at Kenwood, the Lennons' home in Surrey's stockbroker belt. Cynthia adopted the Brigitte Bardot look to please John, but it failed to create lasting domestic harmony. They had drifted apart long before Yoko Ono came on the scene.

Opposite: When the Beatles were on tour, there was invariably a success to toast and a bar provided for the purpose. This picture was taken during the UK tour in the fall of 1964, when the group were putting the finishing touches to *Beatles For Sale*. Their fourth album in 21 months was released in time for the Christmas market, along with the new single, "I Feel Fine". Both went to number one, *Beatles For Sale* displacing *A Hard Day's Night* at the top of the UK album chart.

Above: Card games were a way of relieving the boredom when the boys were waiting to go on stage.

Opposite: The Beatles on location in the Bahamas, where shooting for their second feature film *Help!*, began in February 1965.

Right: Paul in pensive mode during location shooting in the Bahamas. One of his preoccupations during this period was completing a song that he'd been working on for months. His constant tinkering with it on set is said to have driven director Dick Lester to distraction. The melody to "Yesterday" had arrived fully formed when he woke one morning, and he was convinced it was a steal until friends assured him otherwise. The lyrics were the problem, for Paul had used "Scrambled Eggs" as a working title, and it proved difficult to dislodge. He had cracked the problem by June 1965, in time for "Yesterday" to feature on *Help!*, and it went on to become the most recorded song of all time.

Opposite and above: In March 1965 the Beatles swapped the sunny climes of the Caribbean for the Austrian Alps, where the snow scenes for their second film were shot. The movie's working title was *Eight Arms To Hold You*, which even John and Paul thought rather unwieldy as a potential song lyric. When director Dick Lester suggested *Help!*, John dashed off the title song – and the group's next number one – in a matter of hours. Photographer Robert Freeman had the idea of posing the boys so that they spelled out the soundtrack album's title in semaphore on the cover, but rejected it on aesthetic grounds. It actually reads NUJV! Nor was the picture taken against a snowy landscape; it was

Opposite: George is all smiles for this fun photo shoot, but he was the first to rail against the oppressive regime of the touring days. The caged bird metaphor was apposite for band members who had become prisoners of their own success.

Above: The Beatles study the history of Clivedon House, the Berkshire country house which doubled for Buckingham Palace in *Help!*. After filming there on May 10, 1965, the boys rushed to Abbey Road to record a cover version of the Larry Williams song "Dizzy Miss Lizzy". This was primarily for the American market, though the song did eventually make the cut for the *Help!* album. America couldn't get enough Beatles product, a far cry from 1963, when Capitol – EMI's US subsidiary – blithely passed the rights to the early singles on to minor labels, claiming that the Beatles wouldn't succeed over there.

Above: The boys don their best bib and tucker for the premiere of *Help!*. Reviews at the time were mixed, though some of the madcap, comic-book antics have since been much praised, and the Fabs themselves were compared to the Marx Brothers. The soundtrack album was filled with gems, including the chart-topping title track and "Ticket To Ride". It shot to number one within days of its August 6 release and remained there for nine weeks.

Opposite: Caught on camera at Twickenham Studios, where the Beatles filmed many scenes featured in *A Hard Day's Night* and *Help!*. In January 1969 the group began filming *Let It Be* at Twickenham, before the cold and damp forced them to repair to Apple Studios. The uninviting atmosphere mirrored the frosty relations between the band members at that point.

Above: The Beatles take to Chicago's White Sox Park during their second concert tour of America in the summer of 1965. A total of 60,000 people watched the two Chicago shows, while at New York's Shea Stadium they played to 55,000, a world record for a pop concert. The move to huge sporting arenas to accommodate the demand for tickets came at a cost. The shows were impersonal, and the deafening screams drowned out the group's vocal and instrumental efforts. It was the peak of the touring era, but amongst the band members the seeds of dissatisfaction were also sown.

Above: The Beatles, MBE. The band members pondered whether to accept the Establishment award in 1965, eventually deciding that if soldiers could be honored for wartime exploits, they merited theirs for services to entertainment. Some of those soldiers returned their awards in protest, feeling the honor to have been debased. Four years later, in November 1969, John joined them. In the accompanying note he said the action was "in protest against Britain's involvement in the Nigeria-Biafra thing, against our support of America in Vietnam, and against "Cold Turkey" slipping down the charts".

Opposite: Paul and Jane Asher at the 1967 premiere of *Here We Go Round The Mulberry Bush*, one of the seminal films of the Swinging Sixties. Paul declined the offer to write the music for the film, but he had already diversified into this area by composing the score for *The Family Way* the previous year. After the tight-knit early years, the Beatles became increasingly involved in solo projects as the decade wore on.

Above: The Beatles pictured with Motown singer Mary Wells. The Beatles were huge fans of the Detroit sound, and on the strength of Wells's 1964 smash hit "My Guy", they invited her to join their UK tour that fall. The boys' musical heroes were predominantly black, and they were affronted at the thought of playing to segregated audiences when they toured America's Deep South. They laid down an ultimatum to the organizers, an early example of pop stars using their public platform to prick a nation's conscience.

Above: The Beatles at play during a photo shoot. The group took a keen interest in the sleeve artwork of their albums, causing several run-ins with EMI bosses. EMI executives were unhappy about the unsmiling monochrome shot the boys chose for the cover of *With The Beatles*, and they were exasperated at the hefty £2,800 bill for the *Sergeant Pepper* gatefold sleeve. On *Rubber Soul* chance played a part. When photographer Robert Freeman projected the results of the cover shoot onto white card for the group's approval, it tipped back and produced an elongated effect. The distortion appealed to the Beatles, who were dabbling freely with mind-altering substances, and they asked Freeman to use the stretched image on the cover of their sixth album.

Opposite: By 1965 the Beatles had outgrown the cheeky Moptop image and their music had reached new levels of sophistication. *Rubber Soul* was a turning point, offering more interesting and often introspective lyrics, while maintaining the group's unerring ear for a catchy pop tune. Fuzz box, sitar and an Elizabethan-style keyboard solo were just some of the indications of the innovative period ahead.

Above: George and Pattie Boyd tie the knot at Epsom Register Office, January 21, 1966. The couple had met on the set of *A Hard Day's Night*, in which Pattie had a minor role as a schoolgirl in the train sequences. Pattie was instrumental in setting George on the eastward road to spiritual enlightenment, having immersed herself in Indian culture and philosophy before her husband. It was she who brought the teachings of Maharishi Mahesh Yogi and transcendental meditation to the Beatles' attention.

Opposite: Rehearsing in 1965, the year the Beatles stepped up a gear from pop supremos to creative artists bearing comparison to Beethoven. The depth and maturity of *Rubber Soul*, released in December that year, stunned fans and fellow musicians alike. Brian Wilson of the Beach Boys was so blown away by the album that he resolved to try to match it with his own next offering, *Pet Sounds*.

Opposite and above: In the mid-sixties the Beatles blazed a trail that can be regarded as the forerunner to MTV – they began to shoot their own films to promote their new singles. Here, George and John perform "Paperback Writer" in a film shot at EMI on May 19, 1966. Neither the new single nor the B-side, "Rain", featured on the group's new album, continuing the policy of refusing to fleece the fans by making them pay twice for the same material. The new long player in question was *Revolver*, a masterwork which has topped several polls as the best album of all time. The reasons are clear enough. All four were at the top of their game, and they were working as a cohesive unit. By the following year, the early signs of the long fragmentation period would begin to show. It was hardly surprising that an early contender for the album title was *Abracadabra*, such was the magical quality of the 35-minute set.

Left and opposite: In the early days of their creative partnership, John and Paul "wrote in each other's faces". A string of hits was produced by the duo bouncing musical and lyrical ideas off each other. Over time, this method gave way to individual composition, when collaboration was reduced to supplying a lick of polish. Ever since the creation of Northern Songs in 1963, all of the pair's output went out under the Lennon-McCartney banner, irrespective of authorship, but there was a competitive edge between them when it came to the singles market. Each had periods in the ascendancy, and on two memorable occasions their sublime offerings yielded double A-sides. In December 1965 Lennon's "Day Tripper" was paired with McCartney's "We Can Work It Out"; fourteen months later, "Penny Lane" and "Strawberry Fields Forever", Paul and John's respective nostalgia trips, provided what many consider to be a single of unrivaled quality. Amazingly, it stalled at number two in the UK charts, blocked by Engelbert Humperdinck's "Release Me".

Above and opposite: The Beatles on location at Chiswick House in London, where some of the
sequences for the "Paperback Writer"/"Rain" promo were shot. Director Michael Lindsay-Hogg
intercut performance footage with film of the group relaxing in the stately home's walled gardens. The
new single showed John and Paul in top form. McCartney's A-side, with its lyric in the form of an
imploring letter, elevated bass guitar to lead status. He badgered the sound engineers to crank up the
bass level beyond EMI limits, for which they were given a rap over the knuckles. The song was
memorably backed up by Lennon's latest "trippy" offering. The saturated sound on "Rain" was achieved
by recording the rhythm track at a fast speed, then slowing it down on playback. It also featured
backwards guitar and vocals, both of which would become regulars in the group's creative armory.

Above: The Beatles had a very tight inner circle during the tumultuous eight-year period from "Love Me Do" to *Let It Be*. Two members of the loyal entourage are pictured with the band in this informal shot: Mal Evans (left) and Neil Aspinall (far right). Mal's entrée came via his part-time job as Cavern Club doorman. He became a trusted factotum, and also joined in on many recording sessions. He struggled to make the adjustment when the heady days of Beatledom came to an end, suffering bouts of depression. In 1976 Mal was shot dead by Los Angeles police officers who found him brandishing an air gun when they answered an emergency call. Neil Aspinall was a Liverpool Institute schoolmate of Paul and George, giving up a career in accountancy to go on the road with the Beatles. He drove the battered £80 van that was acquired to transport the boys and their equipment to their early gigs, and went on to become Apple's chief executive. He stood down in April 2007 and died a year later.

Opposite: Filming a promo clip at Chiswick House, London, in May 1966.

Opposite: A city gent appears blissfully unaware that he is in the presence of the pop industry's leading lights. Perhaps he would be more impressed if he knew their stock market worth. Northern Songs, the company formed in 1963 to publish Lennon-McCartney songs, was floated on the market two years later. It made them a tidy sum, though not as much as it should, for Brian Epstein had handed a large slice of the cake to music publisher Dick James. John and Paul were incensed when they discovered that they owned only a share of their output; James got richer with every Lennon-McCartney release.

Above: May 19, 1967: the Beatles hold a launch party for their seminal long player, *Sgt. Pepper's Lonely Heart's Club Band*. The group's eighth album might have been very different had George Martin not raided the song bank for a new single at the beginning of the year. The loss of "Penny Lane" and "Strawberry Fields Forever" derailed the idea for an album based around childhood reminiscence, and a new concept took shape. It was Paul's idea for the group to assume the guise of a fictitious band as a way of distancing themselves from the trappings of Beatlemania, with which they had become so disillusioned.

Opposite: *Sgt. Pepper* may be regarded
as Paul's magnum opus, for he was the
creative force behind the landmark
album. George's search for truth and
enlightenment had led to India, and he
had reservations about an album based
on assumed identities. Ringo also had
misgivings, for with the full panoply of
orchestral sounds on display, he felt
like a bit-part player. John criticized the
album for a concept that wasn't
followed through, though he did make
a vital contribution, including "Lucy In
The Sky With Diamonds".
Commentators seized on the "trippy"
lyrics and assumed that the title was
shorthand for LSD. In fact, the
inspiration – and the title – came from
a picture painted by his son Julian.

Left: The Beatles display their album at
the *Sgt. Pepper* launch party. The sleeve,
which won a Grammy, was the first
album cover to have lyrics printed
on it.

Above: Photographer Linda Eastman was among a select few journalists invited to the *Sgt. Pepper* launch party at Brian Epstein's Belgravia home on May 19, 1967 but a year would pass before she and Paul became an item. In July 1968, Paul and Jane Asher finally called time on their foundering relationship, and that fall he invited Linda and daughter Heather to come and stay. Before the year was out, they were inseparable.

Opposite: June 25, 1967: The Beatles perform "All You Need Is Love" to an audience of 400 million in a trans-Continental TV special, *Our World*. The brief was for a simple, catchy song that could cross international boundaries. Paul and John set to work separately, and it was the latter who came up with a song that would become the anthem of the Summer of Love. There was a party atmosphere at Abbey Road on the day of transmission, Mick Jagger, Eric Clapton and Keith Moon among the revelers who backed the Beatles with the singalong refrain.

Opposite: Paul had come up with the idea for this Beatles project: a free-form musical based around the idea of a mystery coach tour. A jolly jaunt round the West Country with a motley cast produced a lot of fun set pieces and – naturally – some great musical interludes. However, the *Magical Mystery Tour* gets off to an inauspicious start when the coach fails to turn up at the appointed time. Paul and poet Ivor Cutler – who played Buster Bloodvessel in the film – are left twiddling their thumbs for a couple of hours, much to the delight of passing autograph hunters and snappers.

Above: The Beatles aboard the Magical Mystery Tour special in September 1967. This was the first Beatles project following the death of Brian Epstein, whose body was discovered at his London home on August 27. The coroner's

Opposite: The Beatles pictured in their hotel room in Teignmouth, Devon, during the filming of *Magical Mystery Tour.*

Above: The Beatles take a breather on Plymouth Hoe during the *Magical Mystery Tour* shoot. The photo call was organized to satisfy the demands of the army of journalists that formed a lengthy train behind the tour bus. The 52-minute film aired that Christmas in black-and-white, which drained much of the surreal enchantment from the magical concept, and it proved too incoherent for most critics' taste. Paul rebutted media criticism by saying that the film was deliberately formless and had been misunderstood.

Above: John and George, along with their wives, stepping out in London to mark the opening of the Apple Boutique on December 7, 1967. The store where "beautiful people can buy beautiful things" was just one branch of an organization that set out to turn accepted corporate wisdom on its head. Profit was not at the heart of the business model; each Apple offshoot was meant to be a liberating enterprise, giving creative people their head. Apple Boutique closed its doors in July 1968, ending a brave eight-month experiment.

Opposite: Ringo and George pose with a Blue Meanie, one of the characters from their 1968 animated feature, *Yellow Submarine*. The Beatles showed little interest in the film, contributing a few fillers from their song stockpile to discharge their contractual duty to the makers. They changed their minds when the charming undersea fantasy hit the screens, for the film became one of the landmark productions of the psychedelic era.

Opposite: John Lennon and Yoko Ono's paths first crossed in November 1966, when the Beatle attended an exhibition the avant-garde artist held at London's Indica Gallery. Until then John was no great fan of conceptual art, but he warmed to the bizarre exhibits – and to their creator. One piece called for the viewer to pay five shillings to climb a ladder and knock a nail into a wall. John said he would knock an imaginary nail in and pay an imaginary five shillings. A connection was made, though it would be another 18 months before the relationship was cemented.

Right: George and Pattie Harrison en route to the 1968 Cannes Film Festival. George had written the soundtrack to the film *Wonderwall*, which was being premiered at the festival. A solo project provided a welcome creative outlet for George, who became increasingly frustrated with the small number of his songs that were making it onto vinyl. At a token rate of one or two tracks per album, Harrison already had a stockpile of material that would take years to air under the Beatles banner. Many songs that fell by the wayside during this period turned up on George's post-break-up triple album, *All Things Must Pass*.

Left: During the fractious *White Album* sessions, George felt undermined more than ever. It was almost two months before a Harrison song took center stage, and after showing such restraint he was determined to assert control over his work. The song in question was "While My Guitar Gently Weeps", inspired by an exercise in randomness. George opened a book, intent on writing a song around the first words he lighted upon. It was an outstanding song but the arrangement proved to be a struggle. After numerous unsatisfactory remakes, he bumped into Eric Clapton and invited him to play on the record. An apprehensive Clapton gave a virtuoso performance, and the presence of the most celebrated session musician ever employed by the Beatles helped thaw a chilly atmosphere.

Opposite: December 11, 1968: John, Yoko and five-year-old Julian Lennon are flanked by Eric Clapton and Brian Jones during the recording of *Rock And Roll Circus*, the Rolling Stones' abortive riposte to *Magical Mystery Tour*. The proposed TV special was never aired, but its significance lay in the fact that John appeared on stage minus the other Beatles for the first time.

Opposite: January 30, 1969: The Beatles' final public performance, the acclaimed rooftop session. The impromptu set stopped the traffic and brought the long arm of the law knocking on the door of the Apple building. Paul had urged them to return to their performance roots – to "get back to where they once belonged" – as a way of mending fences. It was too late for that, but for 42 joyous minutes the world's greatest band was in harmony again.

Above: In January 1969 the Beatles allowed the cameras in to watch them in rehearsal mode. Ideas for a grand performance were floated, but – rooftop concert apart – never materialized. What remained was many hours of studio footage showing a group disintegrating before the viewers' eyes. The project was eventually shelved, and the tapes lay fallow for a year before legendary producer Phil Spector was brought in to rescue an album from the chaos. The sleeve of *Let It Be*, with its black borders, was a fitting way to mark the passing of a fabulous band.

Above: Paul and Linda pictured on their wedding day, March 12, 1969, with Linda's daughter, Heather, holding on tightly to her new step-father. None of the other Beatles was present at the Marylebone Register Office ceremony.

Opposite: John and Yoko tied the knot eight days later in Gibraltar. Neither George nor Ringo was available when "The Ballad Of John And Yoko" was recorded in April, so John and Paul put their differences behind them and shared the vocal and instrumental load. There were studio high jinks as John exhorted Paul on drums, shouting, "Faster, Ringo!", to which he received the reply "OK George." The song hit the top of the charts a week after "Get Back" had been toppled. The Beatles came together that summer for one final hurrah with the recording of *Abbey Road*. All that remained thereafter was the acrimonious legal proceedings to dissolve the greatest band in the history of popular music.